An Angler's Guide To
Paint Creek

Jason Davis

An Angler's Guide To

Paint Creek

Dedication

For Ryan Miller
May you always look down on us from your heavenly trout stream.

About the Author

Jason Davis was introduced to trout fishing over 25 years ago on a small Northern Michigan stream. He began his fishing career with a spinning rod and eventually started fishing exclusively with a fly rod.

Currently, Jason is a Board Member of the Clinton Valley Chapter of Trout Unlimited and an active volunteer with the Clinton River Watershed Council. Taking an active role with these two organization has allowed him to be more aware of the efforts needed to protect the valuable resources we have in our own backyards.

He now lives within a 15 minute drive of Paint Creek and can often be found somewhere along the creek chasing trout. Jason has a wonderful fiancee, a step-son interested in the outdoors, too many fly rods to count, and a desire to help keep Paint Creek growing as an urban trout fishery.

Acknowledgements

Many thanks go out to my fiancee Kelley Sunman, her son Sean, and the rest of my family. Without their acceptance of my angling addiction this guide would have never been possible.

Additional gratitude is due Wayne Snyder, Dan Keifer, Tom Quail, Adam Avery, Tom Jaissle, Jeremy Geist, Shawn Chalker, Brett Watson, Jim Francis, Tim & Michelle Muir, the Clinton River Watershed Council, Oakland County Planning & Economic Development, Al Woody, the Michigan Fly Fishing Club, the Lake Orion Historic Society, and the Rochester Avon Historic Society.

And of course, thanks to the many angling friends who have shared our local waters with me. We have all learned from each other.

Credits

Funding for this project was made possible by the Clinton Valley Chapter of Trout Unlimited, the Vanguard Chapter of Trout Unlimited, the Challenge Chapter of Trout Unlimited, and Brian & Erin Considine on behalf of the Paul H. Young Chapter of Trout Unlimited.

Layout & Design : Jason Davis, Kelley Sunman
Historic Text : Wayne Snyder
Photos : Jason Davis, Adam Avery, Wayne Snyder, Brett Watson
Editing Committee : Wayne Snyder, Tom Quail, Jeremy Geist, Tom Jaissle
Fly Selection : Jason Davis, Tom Jaissle

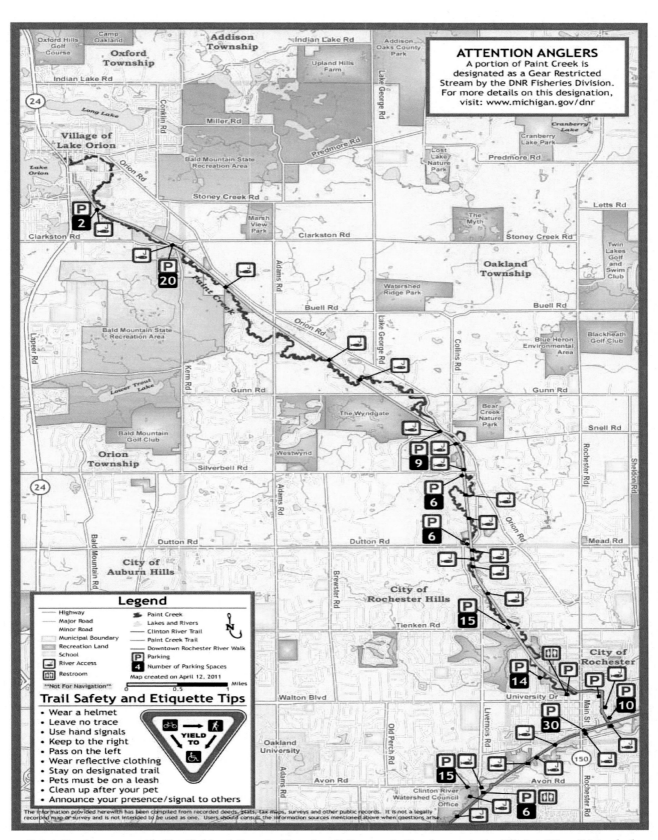

Paint Creek map provided by Oakland County Planning & Economic Development, the Clinton River Watershed Council, the Michigan Fly Fishing Club, and Al Woody of Trout Unlimited.

An Angler's Guide To
Paint Creek

As the sun slowly makes its way through the trees an angler eases into the cool waters of Paint Creek. The morning dew still hangs on the spider webs which span across the creek. A mist of fog rises from the water into the brisk morning air.

While patiently waiting for the first tell-tale sign of a feeding trout a cardinal lands on a nearby tag alder, a chipmunk scrambles across a fallen ash tree, and just downstream a small whitetail deer rises from its morning nap. The Paint Creek corridor is slowly coming to life.

Nature's simple wonders surround the angler just as they would on any Michigan trout stream. Pausing for a moment, the angler reflects where in this great state he is. The short ten minute drive to the creek slowly comes back to him. A smile appears on his face from knowing this gem of a trout stream is so close to home.

Just then the surface is broken by a rising trout. With no apparent hatch in the air the angler searches his fly box for something that may interest this feeding trout. As he looks intently through his flies something crawls across his hand. It is a small ant and just the clue he needs to fool this trout.

After tying on a size 16 parachute ant the angler makes a delicate cast to where the rising trout was last seen. The ant pattern drifts slowly down the creek without the slightest sign that it may be an imposter. With a watchful eye the angler follows the fly through its drift.

Suddenly the surface is broken and the parachute ant is gone. A golden flash lights up the water where the fly once was and the angler quickly sets

A healthy Paint Creek brown trout.

the hook. The fish breaks the surface and performs a beautiful leap. Without losing concentration the angler looks over his shoulder hoping someone may have witnessed this majestic aerial display.

Working patiently to keep the fish hooked the angler slowly brings the fish closer. With one graceful scoop the fish is soon cradled safely in his soft rubber trout net.

As the angler snaps a quick picture a splash is heard just upstream. Looking up, he realizes that another trout is feeding. The smile comes back to his face once he realizes that this just might be one of the best days he has had on Paint Creek.

The magic of Paint Creek has shown itself to yet another angler as it has so many days previously. This magic can be found on many Michigan trout streams but is ever so special on Paint Creek only minutes from home.

A Historic Profile

Paint Creek is a diminutive stream in character and one must think small to fish its sparkling waters. We call it our area's 'Little Gem' so it is hard to fathom that it is also characterized as an urban trout stream. Only forty miles north of Detroit, it is one of only two designated trout streams in Oakland County, the other being the much smaller Trout Creek, which is itself a tributary of Paint Creek.

Streams and rivers have histories and Paint Creek is no exception. All along its flow one can piece together colorful bits of local lore going back almost two hundred years. For the contemplative fisherman, these histories provide a fascinating glimpse into some of the reasons why Paint Creek has remained a favorite backyard fishery for decades.

What we know as Paint Creek truly begins as the outflow from a dam on the eastern side of Lake Orion (the lake), near the downtown district of the Village of Lake Orion. The dam is unique in that it is a conventional over-spill type that was modified with an eighteen inch bottom-draw pipe at the dam's base in 1991. The endeavor was known as Project 30 and the intended effect was to mix cold, deep lake water with the warm surface discharge to maintain a summer downstream water temperature below 70° F.

To test the experiment, brown trout were released immediately below the dam the following year. The trout thrived throughout the summer. As a result of Project 30 it is believed that some five stream miles of new trout habitat were created benefiting not only the fish but cold water aquatic insects like blackflies and stoneflies.

Just outside the Village of Lake Orion near the Kern-Clarkston Road bridge area a man named Joseph Jackson built one of the first creek

powered sawmills to cut logs into board lumber in 1825. Ten years later Powell Carpenter bought the mill and added a grist mill to grind wheat into flour. Powell and his crew also built a general store, a cooper shop, a blacksmith shop, three houses and a school.

In 1865 the complex was purchased by Robert G. Rudd and became known as Rudd's Mill. When the milling operations finally stopped in 1926 all of the buildings were demolished.

The millpond's dam remained intact until 1946 when it was washed out in a monstrous storm, flooding Paint Creek all the way to the village of Rochester. Just to the west of the Kern-Clarkston parking lot there is heavily grafitti'd concrete railroad bridge that dates from 1924.

Just below Clarkston Road the creek is joined in its southeasterly journey by the Paint Creek Trail. The Paint Creek Trail was the first Rail-to-Trail project in the state of Michigan. The Detroit and Bay City Railroad Company built the original rail line in 1872. The track connected Detroit to Bay City and a one-car passenger train went daily north in the mornings and back south in the afternoons until about 1950.

The Michigan Central Railroad later acquired the line and then eventually Penn Central took over the railroad. In 1974 work began to remove the steel

Rudd's Mill once stood on Paint Creek close to the current Clarkston and Kern Road crossing.
Image provided by the Lake Orion Historic Society.

Paint Creek

track, spikes and cross-ties, and the railroad bed was graded and covered with an all-weather surface of crushed limestone. The Paint Creek Trail was opened to the public in 1983 and today it receives over 100,000 visitors annually; among them walkers, joggers, bicyclers, cross-country skiers and, of course, fishermen.

While Paint Creek was seen primarily as an important source of waterpower during the nineteenth century and early twentieth century,

A Detroit United Railroad car sits atop the bridge over Paint Creek.
Image provided by the Rochester Avon Historic Society.

its value as a recreational resource was becoming apparent to some as early as the 1960's. At that time the nation became increasingly aware of water pollution issues due to uncontrolled infusions from residential, agricultural and industrial sources and "environmentalism" became a fashionable and important cause.

Walter P. Reuther, president of the United Auto Workers from 1946 to 1970, was a passionate friend of Paint Creek. After an assassination attempt on his life in 1948 Reuther purchased a cottage home on the creek in 1952. The cottage's discreet location was known only to be somewhere off Orion Road in Oakland Township.

Reuther fell in love with the creek's rich beauty, but became concerned with the increasing water pollution he witnessed there. Alarmed, he called community citizens and activists together and formed the Paint Creek "Citizens Conservation Committee". The primary goal of the committee was to "Restore Paint Creek to its original state of natural purity and beauty…". Reuther was an accomplished fly-fisherman and always carried a portable fly rod in his briefcase on his travels.

Below Gunn Road there was once a large concrete dam on the Iafrate Compound property where, years ago, the owner also maintained a

small herd of elk for his hunting. The dam was privately built and raised the creek level about five feet to form a small millpond. There is a box-flume on the millpond that connects and regulates the flow to the millrace built by Needham Hemingway in 1835.

At Gallagher Road a gristmill was originally established at the current site of the historic Paint Creek Cider Mill and was known as the Goodison Grist Mill. The original mill was built by Needham Hemingway in 1835, in the village of Goodison, then a small hamlet established in 1827.

A half-mile upstream from the mill, Hemingway dammed the creek and dug a millrace to power the turbine that turned the millstones. By 1877, William Goodison had bought Hemingway's mill, enlarged it and installed modern machinery.

The mill operated until 1941. When the milling operations finally stopped, after more than a century of service, the structure was sadly dismantled and the present Paint Creek Cider Mill was built. There was an upscale restaurant in the cider mill from the mid-1980's until 2004.

Near the intersection of Dutton Road and the Paint Creek Trail one will find three old railroad bridges (now part of the Paint Creek Trail) each with faint footpaths along the creek. One of the pools

Paint Creek

here is called Swing Tree. It was once one of those magical summer places where sun-bronzed kids swung on an old tire hung by a rope from the branch of a giant oak and fell gleefully into the pool. The old tree died and fell across the creek many years ago, but fish Swing Tree today and you'll still hear the haunting echoes of the children's laughter.

A short walk downstream from the Rochester Municipal Park in Downtown Rochester will bring you to the historic Paint Creek Tavern with the creek running swiftly and boulder-broken

Avon Park circa 1950 now the Rochester Municipal Park.
Image provided by the Rochester Avon Historic Society.

just alongside the building. The Paint Creek Tavern was established in 1934 by a proprietor named Walter (Brownie) Brown. Young Brownie used to sell apples, popcorn, and caramel corn to passengers while riding the Detroit United (electric) Railway cars down to the South Hill Trestle and back again.

Encouraged by his success Brownie established a beer garden and bar at the present site of the tavern and it is said to have been the first bar in Oakland County to allow the sale of alcohol after Prohibition was rescinded.

In the 50's the bar was named the Paint Creek Yacht Club and membership cards were issued to regulars. Thirsty fishermen today still frequent the old tavern after a hot summer's day of fishing the creek for draughts of cold beer and tasty hamburgers. They've also been known to visit Lipumas Coney Island just across the creek.

Early in the twentieth century, Western Knitting Mills (formerly the Rochester Woolen Mills) built a dam on Paint Creek to raise the water level and create a large pond east of Rochester Road called Chapman Pond. In 1901, the pond was expanded to a 12 acre lake and improvements were made to the existing dam.

These improvements produced a 25 foot water fall which powered the mill until after World War I when generators were installed to provide electric power to the Mill.

On June 18, 1946 a major rainfall caused Rudd's

Western Knitting Mills Dam circa 1909.
Image provided by the Rochester Avon Historic Society.

Paint Creek

Mill (near Lake Orion) to burst. The water from the broken impoundment eventually reached Chapman Pond. This caused the land around the dam to give way and flood eastern Rochester. Several homes and businesses were destroyed in the flood.

Efforts to force the water back into its original channel were unsuccessful. Later that summer the lake was drained and filled in with gravel from a nearby hill. This site is now the home of the Rochester Hills Public Library and will forever be part of Paint Creek's history.

Paint Creek's journey ends rather unceremoniously with its confluence with the Clinton River below Second Street in Rochester. This is also an access site to the Clinton River Trail, another Rail-to-Trail project. Paint Creek both widens and enlarges the Clinton on its own history-fraught odyssey to Lake St. Clair.

In more recent memory the little creek became a tumbling maelstrom in September 2008 when two consecutive days of hard rain raised the water levels to flood stage. The creek's rate of flow had already reached torrential levels when on September 14, 2008, what was left of Hurricane Ike blew north through the region adding a third day of torrential downpours. One could only guess what was happening to the creek's trout - most likely they had all been flushed down to the Clinton River or beyond. The fishing would not recover by the end of trout season September 30th.

If you fish a majestic river, a proud stream or even a pretty little creek long enough, sooner or later you want to know more about it. Paint Creek is one of those addictive streams.

Geological History

Paint Creek's hydrology is strongly influenced by Michigan's rich geological history. Glaciation during the last ice age (Pleistocene Epoch) was the major force that helped form the landscape surrounding the creek.

Roughly 15,500 years ago glaciers covered the state of Michigan. As they flowed over earth's outer crust, the glaciers ground up and transport-

Elevation drops in the creek produce beautiful riffles.

ed large amounts of rock. Melting on the edges of the glaciers caused the thinning ice to deposit ground-up rock beneath the huge mass of ice.

These glaciers often held in one place for very long periods of time (tens to hundreds of years) and rock flowed to its leading edges. The rock then piled up to form large end moraines on the landscape. These end moraines produced some of the most scenic areas in the watershed.

The unsorted mixture of rocks, gravel, sand, and clay deposited by a glacier is called glacial till. Most of the hills surrounding Paint Creek are thick ridges of glacial till. A ground moraine, the flat, low-lying landscape which the melting glacier retreated, consists of a thinner layer of till. Outwash deposits are then formed when sand is eroded, transported, and deposited by melt water streams on the glacier's leading edge.

Deposits of sand and gravel created outwash plains from the numerous melt water streams that flowed away from the glacier. While these outwash deposits often consist of similar material as till, they

An Anglers Guide

Lapeer Road	970 feet
Kern Road	945 feet
Adams Road	890 feet
Gunn Road	845 feet
Orion Road	830 feet
Silver Bell Road	810 feet
Dutton Road	785 feet
Tienken Road	775 feet
Rochester Road	740 feet
Second Street	720 feet

Paint Creek's topography changes dramatically as it flows southeast from Lake Orion to its confluence with the Clinton River. The creek is roughly 15 miles in length and has an elevation drop of approximately 250 feet. The above relief map shows the glacial impacts and the Paint Creek corridor that have developed over time.

are generally better sorted. Both till and outwash deposits have a relatively high permeability that allows for a relatively free flow of ground water.

The glaciers provided an outstanding topography to begin the formation of Paint Creek. Geological features (including terrain and soils), climate changes, and vegetation communities have had a major influence on the landscape we see today.

Soil at the earth's surface is constantly changing. As wind and water erode particles from the surface, weathering and biological activity produces additional soil from the exposed rock. The soil profile that eventually develops is a result of several factors which act together; original material, climate, vegetation, topography, time, and animals, including man. Of course, the primary effect of human interaction is the increased erosion due to man-made land modifications.

Paint Creek begins and ends in glacial outwash sand and gravel yet the middle section of the creek travels through end moraines

of medium-textured till. Glacial deposits surrounding Paint Creek support high ground water conductivity, especially at the creek's upper and lower ends. The middle portion, which flows through medium-textured till, also provides a moderate to good inflow of groundwater.

The original landscape carved out by the glaciers produced a varying topography within Paint Creek's watershed. Over time, this landscape has experienced several changes yet the major effects of the glaciers end moraine deposits are still seen today.

If we look at Paint Creek today we can see the effects the glaciers had on the landscape. For example, the section of the creek that flows through the Bald Mountain Recreational Area is relatively flat and the soil contains mostly sand and gravel. Once the creek approaches Adams Road the surrounding topography greatly changes and the creek is littered with more cobble and boulders than sand.

One of the most telling glacial effects on Paint Creek is the creek's overall elevation drop.

8

Paint Creek

The creek begins at an elevation of roughly 980 feet at the Lake Orion Dam and drops to almost 720 feet at its confluence with the Clinton River. Along the 15 miles of Paint Creek, the elevation drops an average of 17.7 feet per mile. This dramatic drop has produced a swift moving creek with the appropriate hydrology to support an excellent trout fishery.

The combination of the creek's high gradient and good potential for ground water inflow makes this one of Southeast Michigan's best opportunities for a coldwater fisheries management plan. Michigan's Department of Natural Resources has reacted to this by managing Paint Creek as a valuable trout fishery right here in our backyards.

Riparian Corridor

The riparian corridor surrounding Paint Creek affects the creek in different ways. The creek's substrate, in-stream cover, water temperature and water quality are all impacted by the use of the riparian corridor. Changes in land usage occur as the creek flows through the Village of Lake Orion, Orion Township, Oakland Township, Rochester Hills, and Rochester.

In the Village of Lake Orion, Paint Creek's riparian corridor is almost completely covered by medium to low-density residential development. Due to historic development, homes and apartment complexes have been built along the creek. In this area, the riparian cover consists mostly of manicured lawns and residential plantings. A few larger trees can be found on the creek's banks that provide excellent undercuts for trout to call home.

Once the creek flows into Orion Township most of the riparian corridor is less developed, due in large part to the Bald Mountain State Recreation Area. While there is the occasional home along the creek, the riparian buffer zone is often wider than those found in the Village of Lake Orion. This buffer zone is made up of tall wild grasses, shrubs, and larger trees.

As the creek passes the Clarkston and Kern Road crossing, the riparian cover becomes very thick with both native shrubs and invasive buckthorn. This thick cover is excellent at stabilizing the creek banks. Large trees, including oaks, elms, willows, and ash, also add to the natural canopy over the creek. This canopy provides excellent shade to help keep the creek cool during warm summer days.

Further downstream, Paint Creek then enters Oakland Township. For the most part, this township has been successful in maintaining its rural character despite its historic development in Goodison. Just above Adams Road the creek flows through the Cairncross Subdivision and land owners here have maintained some of their banks. However, there is a healthy mix if residential lawns and thick riparian cover along the creek.

As the creek continues through Oakland Township the riparian buffer zone continues to change from very thick wooded areas to manicured lawns. This section of the creek seems to have more willows and ash trees surrounding the creek. Once these trees fall into the creek they provide plenty of woody debris for both the fish and macro invertebrates to call home.

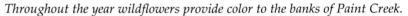

Throughout the year wildflowers provide color to the banks of Paint Creek.

An Anglers Guide

Paint Creek

Continuing downstream, the creek makes its way into Rochester Hills. This community has the largest population of any along Paint Creek and is highly developed with residential homes. Here the riparian buffer zone becomes much smaller and there is an increased number of manicured lawns along the creek.

Downstream from Tienken Road, the creek flows through the Dinosaur Hill Nature Preserve. In this area the riparian land is protected from development and provides the creek with excellent shade and root structure along the creek.

Progressing downstream, Paint Creek flows into Rochester Municipal Park. Here the riparian cover changes dramatically. The park is maintained for recreation use and with the creek located right in the center. To protect the banks of the creek, large rock walls have been constructed along the banks. While there is some riparian growth, it is generally limited to large shrubs and smaller trees.

The creek's final stretch flows through the city of Rochester which has the highest concentration of high-density residential use in the watershed. Despite the heavily developed area around Paint Creek, the riparian buffer zone is in excellent shape. Large trees and thick shrubs provide good root structure along the banks and offer a fair amount of shade to the creek.

As a designated trout stream, Paint Creek flows adjacent to more residential lawns than any of small "northern" Michigan's streams. Manicured lawns and relatively thin riparian cover is not uncommon along Paint Creek's banks. However, an angler wading through many sections of the creek will find it hard to imagine that he is only minutes away from a city as large as Rochester.

A beautifully colored Paint Creek brown trout.

Fish Population

Paint Creek has a trout population that allows local anglers an opportunity to hook a trout within minutes of their home, but this fishery is far more complex than that.

Paint Creek's trout population is the main draw for most local anglers. Historically, the creek once supported brook trout populations, that originated from hatchery stockings. Over the years, the creek experienced many changes that contributed to the loss of these fish today. Most, if not all, of these changes were caused by the ever-growing urbanization surrounding the creek.

In 2001 MDNR sampled several sections of Paint Creek and found that one of the predominant species was brown trout. This is due to many years of stocking efforts by the MDNR Fisheries Division to support the creek's naturally reproducing brown trout population.

Over the years, the brown trout stocking in Paint Creek has gone through several changes. Since 1981 five different strains of brown trout have been stocked. These five strains are the Harrietta, the Plymouth Rock, the Soda Lake, the Wild Rose, and the Gilchrist Creek. Each of these different strains has their own unique characteristics that either prevented their survival in this urban fishery or allowed the strain to flourish.

Beginning in 1981, the Harrietta strain was planted in Paint Creek at seven different locations throughout the creek. From 1981 to 1985 the annual stocking of Harrietta brown trout averaged 5.5 inches in length. Each year an average of 5,148 fish were planted in the creek. This provided an excellent basis for Paint Creek's trout population.

An Anglers Guide

In 1984 MDNR treated the creek with rotenone in an attempt to reduce competition for food in the creek. This resulted in not only the removal of many creek chubs and white suckers but also the creek's brown trout. In an effort to replenish the trout population, MDNR stocked 13,000 Plymouth Rock strain brown trout at seven different locations in the creek.

1986 brought the Soda Lake strain to Paint Creek. This planting of 4,060 fish averaged 5.68 inches in length. During this year another stocking of 200 brown trout occurred at four locations. It is not clear which strain these fish were but they averaged 14.96 inches. This provided Paint Creek with some larger, breeding size brown trout.

The Plymouth Rock strain was once again planted in 1987, but only 1600 fish. This may have been due to reduced quanities of available hatchery fish.

From 1988 to 1991 the Soda Lake strain was stocked at seven different locations along the creek. The stocking of over 22,000 fish averaged 5.52 inches in length.

In 1992 Paint Creek's brown trout stocking was changed to the Wild Rose strain. The first three years this strain was stocked at eight creek locations. The number of stocking locations dropped to five in both 1995 and 1996. Over this five year period, 1992 to 1996, the Wild Rose strain averaged 6.8 inches, over an inch larger than any of the previously planted strains. Average plantings of over 5,700 Wild Rose strain brown trout were planted each year.

From 1997 to 2003 Paint Creek's annual brown trout stocking was a combination of the Wild Rose strain and the Gilchrist Creek strain. 2,800 of each strain were stocked annually at five different locations. The stocked Wild Rose strain averaged 6.32 inches in length while the Gilchrist Creek strain averaged only 4.61 inches in length.

By 2004 MDNR made the decision to stock only the Gilchrist Creek strain in Paint Creek. Since then the creek has received an annual average stocking of approximately 6,000 fish with average length of 5.68 inches.

One may assume that through trial and error MDNR has found an appropriate strain of brown trout for Paint Creek. The Gilchrist Creek strain has been able to withstand the creek's warmer summer months and also reproduce naturally once established in the creek. These fish also exhibit excellent growth rates which provide angler's some very exciting fishing each year.

During the first two weeks of the trout opener, anglers should not be shocked to find spawning steelhead in the lower sections of Paint Creek. These fish migrate up the Clinton River into the creek. This is an angler's best chance at landing a fish in Paint Creek that can be measured in pounds instead of inches.

Annually brown trout are stocked at different locations along Paint Creek.

Paint Creek

The author intently working a run above Tienken Road.

Because of the spawning steelhead it is not uncommon to find small rainbow trout in the lower sections of the creek. These fish have never been stocked in the creek and, most likely, are all naturally reproduced steelhead. They are generally smaller than the brown trout but are eager to take a fly. Anglers fishing in Rochester Park should not be surprised to land several of these fish in a day's outing.

There are several species of fish, other than trout, that make up Paint Creek's fish community. Some of the various smaller species include mottled sculpins and dace. These smaller fish make excellent food for the brown trout. Both sculpins and dace are cold water species and do well in Paint Creek.

The creek also has a large population of creek chubs and white suckers. Anglers fishing small nymphs will often find themselves catching several creek chubs while searching for trout. At times, these fish can be so thick in certain holes that it seems best to move to another section. While these fish can appear as a nuisance they provide another important food source for the large resident brown trout in Paint Creek.

Due to the inputs from Lake Orion, Trout Creek, and other warmer tributaries anglers may find the occasional panfish in Paint Creek. During the warmer summer months when the trout are laying low in cold water pockets it is not uncommon to find multiple panfish in the deeper, slower holes throughout the creek.

Paint Creek Trail

As recently as 1974, the Paint Creek Trail was a railroad corridor. The original rail line was built in 1872 by the Detroit and Bay City Railroad Company and was acquired by Michigan Central Railroad in the late 1890s.

At this time the mile-marking system along the trail was developed. These markers are still found along the trail in the form of metal, diamond-shaped signs at each half mile interval. Each of the markers represents the distance in miles from the center of Detroit to that point.

Today the Paint Creek Trailways Commission (PCTC) owns and manages the Paint Creek Trail as an 8.9 mile linear park. The PCTC's

Paint Creek

An Anglers Guide

mission is to "provide trail users a natural, scenic, and educational experience while preserving the ecological integrity of the Paint Creek Trail for the enjoyment of future generations."

The Paint Creek Trail has an all-weather surface of crushed limestone and is preferred by many trail users due to its natural feel and setting. The limestone is an environmentally friendly surface which is important due to the trails close proximity to Paint Creek.

The trail was the first Rail-to-Trail in Michigan and has remained open to the public since 1983. Annually over 100,000 visitors use the trail as it traverses through Rochester, Rochester Hills, Oakland Township, Orion Township, and the Village of Lake Orion.

Aside from the recreational opportunities the Paint Creek Trail offers (such as jogging, biking, hiking, and cross-country skiing), anglers also find the trail to be a major asset. There are seven locations along the trail which provide excellent access to Paint Creek. They are at Clarkston & Kern Roads, Gallagher Road, the Paint Creek Trail Office on Orion Road, Silver Bell Road, Dutton Road, Tienken Road, and at the Rochester Municipal Park.

Another benefit of the Paint Creek Trail is the miles of streamside access between the various road crossings. Along the trail there are several locations where the creek directly parallels the trail that provide easy access to the creek.

There are also several bridges on the trail that cross Paint Creek. Most of these locations provide maintained angler access points that have been constructed by either the trail commission or the local Trout Unlimited chapters. All of this provides anglers with access to enter and exit the creek without trespassing on private property.

Access Points

Aside from the road crossing parking lots along the Paint Creek Trail, there are several places for anglers to enter and exit Paint Creek. In many locations the Paint Creek Trail is only several feet away from the creek. This provides additional access to the creek. However, entering the creek at random locations may cause additional erosion and sediment load in the creek.

It is important to remember that a large percentage of Paint Creek flows through private property. While anglers can legally fish Paint Creek, respect must be given to property owners. Anglers should remain in the creek and stay off privately owned creek banks unless an obstruction proves dangerous and impassible.

Anglers that respect property owner rights and are courteous when talking with land owners may possibly gain valuable friendships with those living along the creek.

The author and his fishing buddy on the Paint Creek Trail.

Paint Creek

Lake Orion to Clarkston/Kern

The trout fishery on Paint Creek begins in the Village of Lake Orion below the Lake Orion Dam. This dam is a typical overflow structure which helps to maintain seasonal lake levels in Lake Orion. To help maintain Paint Creek's cool to cold water status a bottom draw was installed at the dam in 1991. It is not uncommon to find trout hanging out in the cold water outflow from the bottom draw during the warm summer months.

In the Village of Lake Orion there are two public parks which provide access to Paint Creek. The first, Children's Park, holds many large trout during the early part of trout season. This is a great location to take a child to catch his first Paint Creek trout.

As the creek continues through the Village of Lake Orion the substrate consists primarily of sand with occasional cobble riffles.

Land owners in this section of Paint Creek manicure their banks right down to the creek which contributes to the excessive sand in the creek.

The creek remains relatively void of structure until the Goldengate Avenue crossing. From here the creek continues to wind its way through various backyards. The riparian cover here becomes very thick and the overhanging vegetation provides great cover for wary trout.

Upstream from the historic Rudd's Mill site a well worn path begins to follow the creek bank. This section provides excellent public access and plenty of opportunity for catching a trout. Below the Rudd's Mill site, a series of log jams in relatively shallow water provides good cover for small trout.

Once the creek flows under the Paint Creek Trail the angler will find a short section of the creek with lots of woody debris. While this section often looks worthy of skipping over, it rarely fails to produce a trout.

Lake Orion Dam in downtown Lake Orion at the beginning of Paint Creek's trout waters.

A beautiful section below the historic Rudd's Mill site.

Clarkston/Kern to Adams

The Clarkston Road access site is one of the most popular on Paint Creek. This may be due to its proximity to downtown Lake Orion or due to the excellent public access provided here for local anglers. This is also the only access site that has restrooms available for both trail users and anglers.

Directly below the Clarkston Road bridge, the creek begins to cascade through several riffles and bounce off the piles of woody debris. This section provides plenty of oxygen and lots of cover for a wonderful population of brown trout. While the fish may be smaller on average, the savvy angler can expect plenty of action.

Once the creek travels under the Paint Creek Trail it winds its way through various private land parcels. Tag alders begin to crowd the creek and they provide great cover for trout. Several privately owned bridges span across the creek. A respectful angler should remain in the creek as much as possible as all of these bridges can be walked under.

There is an additional angler access site south of the Paint Creek Trail bridge. At this location a set of stairs had made traversing down the steep bank very easy. This access point provides the angler with a four hour trip back up to Clarkston Road.

Eventually Paint Creek flows behind the Royal Oak Archers Club. In this section casting is almost impossible due to the riparian growth. Excessive amounts of woody debris continue until the creek enters the Cairncross Subdivision. Here the angler will find himself fishing along property owner's backyards until the Adams Road bridge. While this section may appear too developed to support trout, the angler will be pleasantly surprised by probing the deep pools and various undercut banks.

Adams to Gunn

The Adams Road to Gunn Road section is often difficult for the average angler to fish. One of the limiting factors here is the absence of public parking close to either road crossing. In order to fish this section an angler must be prepared for a long walk to and from the creek.

Once in the creek at Adams Road, the angler will find plenty of woody debris and a substrate composed of cobble, gravel, and sand. The banks of the creek are slightly grown over, impeding casting at times. The angler should focus on the deeper runs and undercut banks to locate trout.

Just upstream from the Trout Creek confluence, Paint Creek flows through a heavily manicured section of private property. These land owners have done an outstanding job preventing erosion through this section of the creek.

Eventually the creek makes its way under the Paint Creek Trail. This section provides the angler with some very challenging log jams to navigate. This may be the most woody debris found in any section of Paint Creek. While all of this woody debris makes for difficult casting there are plenty of opportunities to locate large trout under the creek's submerged structure.

Above the Ellamae Bridge crossing, Paint Creek once again flows through backyards of

Paint Creek

various private property owners. From here to the historic Reuther Estate, the creek holds several log jams, undercut banks, deep pools, and lots of overhanging vegetation that all hold the opportunity to hook a very large trout.

After navigating through one of the creek's deepest holes, the angler will find himself winding through several backyards prior to reaching Gunn Road. This section offers some very good fishing in close proximity to Gunn Road.

Gunn to Silver Bell

One of the most unique sections of Paint Creek exists between Gunn and Silver Bell Roads. This section is rich with history and diverse habitat that many trout call home.

At Gunn Road the creek is completely surrounded by private land. With the closest access point downstream at Gallagher Road this is a section that is often overlooked by the average angler. Here the creek begins as a swift moving riffle before it turns into a very slow moving, deep section

of the creek. Combine the soft substrate with large amounts of woody debris and the stage is set for even the most experienced wader to have difficulty.

Downstream from the start of the historic Mill Race, the creek flows over a small dam. Above the dam the substrate is very soft and wading is difficult. This section often holds several trout. Once the creek flows over the dam it gains speed prior to beginning a section that was historically channelized. Here anglers will find plenty of overhanging vegetation harboring an excellent concentration of trout.

After the Gallagher Road crossing the creek regains its sinuosity and collects plenty of woody debris behind the Paint Creek Cider Mill. In this section you will find the in-flow of Gallagher Creek, the last remaining tributary to have documented brook trout. During the spring high water it is not unusual to hear reports of the occasional brookie being caught below this confluence.

The creek then travels under Orion Road and begins a loop through private property. This loop provides several riffles, runs and pools for large trout to hide. Anglers interested in photog-

The Paint Creek Cider Mill

Paint Creek

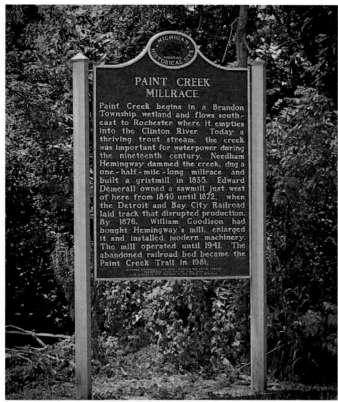

Remembering the historic Mill Race

Silver Bell to Dutton

One of the first things apparent at the Silver Bell Road access site is the Clinton Valley Trout Unlimited Paint Creek Restoration sign. In the mid 1980's Clinton Valley TU spent many man hours restoring this section of Paint Creek. Their work included bank stabilization and building lunker structures. These efforts produced some of the best habitat for holding large trout.

From Silver Bell Road to the first bridge on the Paint Creek Trail, the creek twists and turns its way through various sections of private property. However, this is one section of Paint Creek in which the riparian corridor has been left intact. This may be due to the distance between land owner's homes and the creek.

Several log jams and deep pools provide excellent habitat for large trout. The substrate here is mostly cobble, gravel, and sand. There are also several sections of silt scattered throughout the creek that is perfect habitat for large burrowing mayflies, trout food.

Once Paint Creek flows under the Paint Creek Trail some dramatic changes take place. The creek winds through various log jams yet the water depth remains quite shallow. This section is reminiscent of a Northern Michigan brook trout stream with woody debris scattered throughout. While this section seems to hold very few trout there are plenty of undercut banks that may harbor lunker brown trout.

When the creek flows back under the

raphy will find a beautiful bridge that crosses the creek. Prior to flowing back under Orion Road, a large riffle provides excellent oxygen levels and a plethora of aquatic insects for trout to dine on.

Once Paint Creek crosses back under Orion Road there is an angler access point off the Paint Creek Trail. This access point is within walking distance of both Silver Bell and Gallagher Roads. It is a fine spot to begin the short journey downstream to Silver Bell Road.

From here the creek's morphology begins to change abruptly from deep pools to riffles. This causes one of the most picturesque riffle reaches along the creek. These riffles are home to the most condensed population of rainbow trout in Paint Creek and the deep pools also hold very healthy brown trout.

Just upstream from Silver Bell Road the creek begins to parallel the Paint Creek Trail as it becomes a very non-descript section of water with very high banks and little structure for fish. However, anglers may be surprised by hooking a nice trout within mere yards of the road crossing.

Honoring CVTU's work on the creek.

Paint Creek Trail it again transforms into a promising trout stream. The creek gains plenty of depth and gives the angler the feeling that huge trout could be lurking in every pool.

On the east side of Paint Creek several homes border the creek. Livernois Road land owners are privileged to have a very scenic section of creek in their backyards. Due to the extreme turns along the creek, these land owners have constructed various erosion control structures to keep the substrate of the creek free of sediment.

It is important to note that this section often remains cooler in hot weather due to several overflow wells that flow into the creek. A savvy angler would pay close attention to these well inlets.

For a third time, Paint Creek flows under the Paint Creek Trail. Here the creek seems to gain even more depth as the substrate changes to predominately gravel, sand, and silt. Several log jams provide excellent habitat for both aquatic insects and large trout. There is also plenty of overhanging vegetation that provides homes for terrestial insects, great food for trout.

Prior to reaching Dutton Road, the creek deepens even further as it flows into a huge log jam. The substrate here is very soft and even an experienced angler should take caution. Remember, even

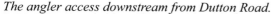

The angler access downstream from Dutton Road.

the largest trout is not worth falling in the creek for.

Once the creek reaches Dutton Road the substrate again changes back to cobble, gravel and sand. A small trail on the east side of the creek leads to the public parking lot on Dutton Road. Here the angler can safely enter and exit Paint Creek.

Dutton to Tienken

The Dutton Road access site is located between Livernois Road and Paint Creek. This small parking lot provides room for six to seven vehicles. During summer weekends the lot is quick to fill up.

Between the Dutton Road bridge and the Paint Creek Trail, the creek begins with a very picturesque rock riffle followed by a rather large log jam. This section of the creek has excellent public access and contains just enough good water to possibly catch a trout or two.

Once Paint Creek flows under the first of three bridges, the makeup of the creek is perfect for holding large trout. The substrate of the creek changes from cobble and gravel riffles, to deep sand and silt bottom pools. Through the years, many trees have fallen into the creek. Over time, woody debris has collected on these trees. These log jams have created some very deep, slow moving sections of the creek.

While the east side of the Paint Creek Trail is primarily private land, it is often the most frequented section of the creek. There are various trails along the edges of the creek that have been worn down by anglers. It is important to note that continued usage of these streamside trails has added to excessive bank erosion. Anglers should use caution here and respect property owner's creek banks.

Once the creek flows under the trail for the second time it begins winding its way through several sections of private property. There are some excellent undercut banks here that potentially hold very large trout. Landowners have maintained the creek well through this section and have left the right amount of woody debris.

When walking this section of Paint Creek

Paint Creek

upstream the angler can see an obvious elevation drop. At times the creek appears to drop over five feet in as short as fifty yards. This provides the creek an increased inflow of oxygen and excellent habitat for both stoneflies and mayflies.

Eventually, the creek flows through a long section that is slowly recovering from past channelization. Through this section, the Paint Creek Trail is rather close to the east bank of the creek and the west bank is privately owned by residents along Livernois Road. This section is slow moving and simply does not have the correct habitat to hold many trout.

The amount of woody debris in the creek increases once the creek regains its sinuosity. While the creek still flows through backyards, this section provides the angler with some very scenic water to fish and plenty of trout.

As the angler wades down to Tienken Road, he will notice the creek becomes wider and shallower over the cobble riffles. Through the upper King's Cove section, there is an absence of woody debris and fish habitat. To combat this, several Eagle Scouts have partnered with the Clinton River Watershed Council to install half log structures. This has been a rewarding and beneficial way for local Scouts to help protect Paint Creek's fantastic fishery.

An upstream view from Dutton Road.

Just prior to the Tienken Road crossing, the creek begins to gain depth as more woody debris is evident. This section provides excellent habitat for trout. From here to the Tienken Road bridge, anglers should be cautious wading as the substrate becomes slippery and the pools may be deeper than expected.

Tienken to Rochester

Tienken Road Bridge is one of the most heavily traveled road crossings along Paint Creek. Here anglers will find easy access to a very productive section of the creek.

As the creek flows through this residential area the substrate is composed of cobble, gravel, and some large boulders. A sequence of riffles and deep pools make for difficult wading while providing excellent habitat for trout.

Public access increases once the creek enters the Dinosaur Hill Nature Preserve. An angler access point on the Paint Creek Trail marks the upstream end of the nature preserve. Here anglers will find great trails along the creek and an easy section to wade.

The Dinosaur Hill section of the creek provides an urban nature experience that is worth keeping your camera at the ready. Anglers should be prepared to share this area with various wildlife, including many whitetail deer.

Eventually, the creek flows under the Paint Creek Trail and through an apartment complex. This section can be difficult to wade due to a deep pool and a series of fast riffles.

Paint Creek then travels under Ludlow Street where it enters the Rochester Municipal Park. Due to excellent access, the park is the most heavily fished section of Paint Creek. Even with tremendous angling pressure, fish are caught on a regular basis.

Throughout the park anglers will find great habitat for holding trout. There are plenty of rock riffles producing additional oxygen for

Paint Creek

In the Rochester Municipal Park several walking bridges cross Paint Creek.

the creek, undercut banks, and deep pools. There are also several bridge crossings to make fishing easy for those who do not wish to wear waders. For a highly urbanized area, this section of Paint Creek holds a surprising number of large trout.

One of the most intriguing aspects of fishing the Tienken to Rochester Road section occurs in the spring. Early in the season lake run steelhead make their way into Paint Creek to spawn. The success of this natural reproduction is evidenced mid-summer by large populations of steelhead smolt occupying several pools in the park.

The excellent rock riffles in the park are also home to some of the most reliable mayfly hatches in all of Paint Creek. It is not uncommon for anglers to find a good sulphur or blue winged olive hatch, trout food.

Downstream from the park the creek flows through several riffles and pools. There are also many undercut banks that hold large trout.

The Paint Creek Trail then crosses the creek just upstream of the Rochester Road Bridge.

Rochester to Clinton River

As Paint Creek flows under Rochester Road it quickly plunges into a deep, fast run that holds several large trout. The elevation drop here is great for adding oxygen to the creek and the boulders scattered throughout the creek provide ex-

A great Paint Creek brown caught by Brett Watson.

25

Paint Creek

An Anglers Guide

cellent cover. It is not surprising, that every year anglers hook multiple large trout in this section.

The substrate below Rochester Road consists primarily of cobble and gravel with the occasional boulder. This makes for some great mayfly and stonefly habitat. Anglers often fish this section during hatches that come close to mimicking hatches of "up north" streams.

Soon, Paint Creek flows behind the Rochester Hills Public Library. From here the creek experiences the most urbanization within its total fifteen mile length. While there are no tributaries that flow into the creek here, there are storm water inflows that provide additional water to Paint Creek. This is a primary reason that the lower creek area is so affected by storm events.

Once the creek makes its final turn south the riparian cover along the creek begins to slightly thin out and there is less overhanging vegetation to obstruct casting. Even though there is very little woody debris in this section, trout use the undercut banks and deep runs for security.

Anglers may find the Rochester Hills Public Library to University section difficult to wade. The heavy amounts of large cobble and

broken concrete in the stream increase the need for studded boots, even during low flow periods.

This section of the creek is the location of the historic Chapman Pond. While fishing here, the thought of standing in, what once was, an old 12 acre pond, may be intriguing.

After University the creek flows through a very picturesque section along the Royal Park Hotel. Anglers will find great habitat on the west side of the creek and an excellent hole directly upstream from the historic Western Knitting Mill dam.

This dam does not have a dramatic elevation drop, unlike alot of dams. Instead, it is built with a ramp section for the creek to flow over. The pressure from this concentration of water has created an excellent hole below the dam that many trout call home.

From here, the creek remains relatively straight until it passes under Second Street. Anglers will find plenty of overhanging vegetation above Second Street. This vegetation provides cover for both brown trout and spring steelhead.

Below Second Street, Paint Creek makes its final run before its confluence with the Clinton River. This section provides swift current and plenty of holding water for resident trout.

Prior to reaching the Clinton River, Paint Creek moves swiftly through Rochester.

Paint Creek

Prior to reaching the Clinton River, Paint Creek flows under the Clinton River Trail Bridge. Early season anglers often use this access site to search for spring steelhead.

Hatches

Paint Creek, like any other trout stream, has an annual sequence of hatches that the trout key on. However, the creek's hatches can be somewhat unpredictable. During trout season there are ten different insect hatches anglers need to be aware of.

As with any other cold water stream with good water quality, Paint Creek experiences a decent early season black stonefly hatch. While this hatch is often fairly sporadic, trout are willing to take a well presented stonefly imitation. Look for stoneflies to hatch in areas where the substrate is larger cobble and coarse gravel. These insects prefer swift moving currents, therefore imitations should be fairly buoyant.

Fly fishing is almost synomous with the grace and beauty of the mayfly. Paint Creek provides anglers the opportunity to fish four different mayflies throughout the trout season.

In late April, the blue-winged olives begin to make their appearance. Weather permitting, this hatch can last most of the season with

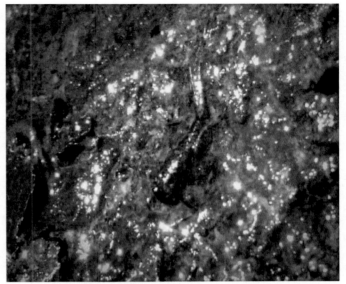

Mayfly nymphs are very common in Paint Creek.

the highest concentrations in early May and late July. These insects are often very small and difficult to see. However, trout see them and they make excellent meals for hungry trout.

Beginning in mid May, both sulphurs and march browns will start to emerge. These mayflies often hatch very close to dusk and their spinner falls occur well after dark. Anglers will not find these hatches everywhere on the creek, yet once they are located they can be very thick and attract very large fish to the surface.

The last of the mayfly hatches on Paint Creek is often the most elusive. For those who enjoy being on the creek at first light, the month of August may be the year's best time to fish. Anglers may be lucky enough to locate a short Trico hatch and get very large fish to rise to very small flies.

The caddis fly is the most common insect found in Paint Creek. Anglers that enjoy inspecting rocks in the creek will not find this surprising. It is not uncommon to find several caddis larva on each rock picked up.

There are three major caddis hatches on the creek each year. The little black caddis is often the first to emerge, followed by the larger grannom caddis, and finally the net-building caddis. Each of these insects has its own color characteristics yet they all seem to prefer the same

A mid-summer sulphur found by Brett Watson.

An Anglers Guide

March Brown	**Peacock Midge**	**Parachute Sulpher**
Double Midge Cluster	**Stimulator**	**X Caddis**
Hare's Ear	**Copper John**	**Zug Bug**
Prince Nymph	**White Scud**	**Pheasant Tail**
Flying Ant	**Foam Monster Hopper**	**Parachute Ant**
Muddler Minnow	**Royal Coachman**	**Muddler Matuka**
Zonker	**Zoo Cougar**	**Krystal Bugger**

basic habitat. These hatches can be some of the thickest of the year and really get trout excited.

One hatch that is often overlooked on Paint Creek is the midge hatch. During the warmer days of summer anglers will find themselves swatting away small blackflies and mosquitos while fishing. These insects may be very small but they attract plenty of trout to the surface. Anglers will need to fish very small flies and light tippets to make this a productive hatch.

Due to the large amount of overhanging vegetation along the creek, the ant "hatch" can be very productive. Each year when the mayflies and caddis are not hatching with consistency, the dry fly angler can turn to a flying ant pattern. Casting these flies under overhanging vegetation during the dog days of summer is often the most productive method.

From late July to the end of September, anglers that enjoy throwing large flies can turn to hopper patterns. This takes the finesse out of laying down a dainty dry fly but is certain to get the attention of Paint Creek's largest trout. These flies are often most productive in areas with high grass along the creek's banks and a slight undercut, for trout to lay in waiting.

When the trout are not rising to dry flies, anglers can drift a nymph along the streambed. To select the proper nymph, simply inspect the rocks or woody debris in the creek, find a crawling insect, and pick a nymph resembling as close to the live bug as possible. Dead drifting nymphs along the bottom of the creek can produce fish at times when it seems the trout are simply not feeding.

Nymphing can be done by either "high sticking' weighted nymphs through deep runs or by adding an indicator. Both methods are productive, yet during low, clear water trout are often spooked by the presence of an indicator.

The one "hatch" anglers should not forget is the streamer "hatch". Paint Creek has a large population of small baitfish and a good streamer can entice large trout anytime during the season.

Streamer selection is not a complicated issue, yet anglers tend to make it difficult. There are two rules to follow for selecting streamers. On days with bright skies and very clear water anglers should select brightly colored flies. Days that are cloudy or when the water is stained, a dark colored streamer usually produces best.

Catch & Release

Michigan fishing regulations allow for legal harvesting of trout in Paint Creek. Creel lim-

Paint Creek Hatch Schedule

Insect	April	May	June	July	August	Sept.	Fly Size
Black Stonefly	■						Size 14-16
Blue Winged Olive		■	■	■	■		Size 16-20
Little Black Caddis		■	■	■	■	■	Size 16-18
Grannom		■	■	■	■	■	Size 14-16
Net-building Caddis			■	■	■	■	Size 16-18
March Brown			■	■			Size 12-14
Sulpher Dun			■	■	■		Size 16-18
Terrestrial - Ants			■	■	■	■	Size 14-18
Terrestrial - Hoppers				■	■	■	Size 6-10
Midges			■	■	■	■	Size 18-24
Trico					■	■	Size 20

An Anglers Guide

its have been established by Michigan Department of Natural Resources fisheries biologists to ensure that quality fishing experiences continue on the creek. However, releasing the majority of our catch will help to maintain and improve the quality fishery we have today. A couple of small trout may make a fine meal but an angler might consider allowing a Paint Creek trout to survive while bringing home a stringer of panfish from one of Oakland Counties public lakes.

Successful release of a fish begins once the fish is hooked. It is important that a fish is not played to exhaustion, land it quickly. Today's fluorocarbon tippet materials allow the angler to use heavier line without spooking fish. This allows for faster landing and less stress on fish.

When playing a fish use lateral pressure instead of lifting a fish directly to the surface. This will allow the fish to tire quicker and become eventually easier to net. It will also prevent fish from coming unhooked by not "prying" the hook out of the fish's mouth.

Signs along Paint Creek promoting Catch & Release.

The net used to land a trout is very important to the survival of a trout. Old style nets with knotted baskets often harm fish while newer rubberized nets are smoother and less harmful to the fish.

Once netted always handle trout as little as possible. Be sure to wet your hands if you must touch the fish. Keeping a trout in the water until release is important for its survival.

Every trout fisherman should carry a pair of forceps to make hook removal easier. Manually removing a hook can be hard on a fish and using forceps makes the process much easier for both the fish and the angler. Using barbless hooks will also aide in easy hook removal.

Generally, a fish will swim off on its own after being released but if it needs some help always take the time to do so. Gently holding the fish facing upstream is often all that is needed to revive a tired trout.

Releasing a fish you worked all day for can be a humbling experience. Simply taking a picture and imagining the smile on the next lucky angler's face is often enough to make the sight of a healthy fish swimming away rewarding.

This brown was caught and released in late August of 2011.

Paint Creek

Protect, Reconnect, Restore, Sustain

Vanguard Chapter, Trout Unlimited

Increasing the coldwater fishing opportunities throughout Michigan with particular emphasis on our home waters of Paint Creek and the Clinton River.

www.vanguardtu.org

Clinton Valley Chapter, Trout Unlimited

Ensuring our local rivers remain healthy for wild and native fish, and for future generations to enjoy.

www.clintonvalleytu.com

Paul H. Young Chapter, Trout Unlimited

Dedicated to conserving, protecting and restoring Michigan's coldwater fisheries for over 48 years.

www.paulyoungtu.org

Challenge Chapter, Trout Unlimited

Publishers of the
Trout Angler's Guides

A series of guide maps of
several Michigan rivers.

Order At: www.challengechapter.org

Paint Creek

"I don't know exactly what fly-fishing teaches us, but I think it is something we need to know."
John Gierach

Southeast Michigan's Premier Guide Service
Enriching the lives of anglers and outdoor enthusiasts of all ages.

www.thedownstreamdrift.com

Notes

Notes

34058417R00028

Made in the USA
Middletown, DE
06 August 2016